Jurassic Park Cookbook

Recipes Even Dinosaurs Would Love

By: Susan Gray

© 2020 Susan Gray, All Rights Reserved.

///

License Notices

The author reserves all rights to this publication. No part may be copied, stored, or distributed in any form with the prior written permission of the author.

The author has ensured that the content of this material is accurate and correct. As such, the author is not liable to misuse on the part of the reader or misinterpretation of the text and the effects that may occur.

///

Table of Contents

Introduction 5

   1. Ornithomimus Twice Fried chicken 7

   2. Ankylosauria Veggie pie 9

   3. Jurassic Park Spicy Goat Soup 12

   4. T-Rex BBQ Steak 14

   5. Brachiosaurus Broccoli and cauliflower Salad 16

   6. Jurassic Park Beef Jerky 18

   7. Stegosaurus Ox Tail Stew 20

   8. Carnotaurus Meat Loaf 22

   9. Compsongnathus German Bratkartoffeln-Pan-fried Potato 24

   10. Roasted summer Vegetables Soup 26

   11. Baryonyx Tempura Battered Fried Fish 28

   12. Hadrosaurids pan and oven roasted crunchy Skin Duck Breast 30

   13. Abelisaurus Chicken Kebab 32

   14. Albertosaurus Meat and Veggies Sauce 34

   15. Coelophysis Mini Cookie Nibbles 36

16. Jurassic Park Spicy Chicken Wings 38

17. Allosaurus Squid and spaghetti recipe 40

18. Dinosaurs Eggs Caramel Marshmallow Coated Rice Crisp 42

19. Apatosaurus Berries and Yogurt delight with crunchy nut toppings 44

20. Archaeopteryx Oven Roasted Chicken 46

21. Deinonychus chicken feet snack 48

22. Diplodocus Hummus Dipping Sauce 50

23. Dinosaur Braised beef shanks 52

24. Giganotosaurus Banoffee Pie 54

25. Minmi White Chocolate chips Cupcake 56

26. Spinosaurus BBQ Baby Back Pork Ribs 58

27. T-Rex Stir-fry Shrimps 60

28. Troodon Baked Nut Crusted Salmon 62

29. Dinosaur shaped cookies 64

30. Jurassic Park Adult Cocktail 66

Conclusion 68

About the Author 69

Author's Afterthoughts 70

Introduction

When we think Jurassic park, we imagine meat, well-seasoned, medium-rare or cooked, your choice, meat drizzled with sweet delicious gravy sauce that melts in your mouth. Well, yes, after all, the dinosaurs were mostly carnivores. Okay, we will add some vegetables, only to ensure we have enough fiber in our diet.

However, you like your meat and veggies cooked, we are sure you will love this, and the dinosaurs would enjoy this if we invited them for dinner or through a drive-through.

Get your pen and paper and be ready to enjoy meals that will have you fall in love with your butcher at the local mart.

So, if you are ready, these are 30 recipes for the dinosaur friend you have or in you, cook, and learn more about the dinosaurs.

1. Ornithomimus Twice Fried chicken

These ostrich look-alike dinosaurs have feathers all over, run very fast with long legs to cover large distances.

Serves 4

Cook Time 40 minutes

Ingredients

- 1 whole chicken cut into pieces
- 1 tsp paprika
- 1 tsp garlic powder
- 1 tsp ginger powder
- 1 tsp chili flakes
- 1 tsp dill, oregano, and thyme
- 1 tsp chicken seasoning
- 500 ml of chicken stock
- Oil to fry

Method

Cook chicken with all the ingredients except for the oil

Let the chicken be cooked but firm

Remove from the liquid, allow it to dry out a bit, and then fry in hot oil

When the sizzle has died down, remove, heat the oil again

Deep fry the chicken until crispy and golden brown

serve

2. Ankylosauria Veggie pie

This armored dinosaur has a design that looked like the lattice on a pie, and we are sure they would like this recipe.

Serves 8

Cook Time 45 minutes

Ingredients

- 1 pack store-bought pie dough
- 2 cups chopped carrots
- 2 cups chopped celery
- 3 cup small diced potatoes
- 1 tbsp oil
- 1 tsp garlic, oregano, and thyme
- 1 tbsp flour
- ½ cup of milk
- Salt and pepper to taste
- 1 egg beaten to brush

Methods

In a hot non-stick pan, add the oil, carrot, celery and potatoes, a sprinkle of salt and pepper and allow it to cook until soft but firm about 7 minutes

Thaw the pastry dough. Cut into rounds that will fit an already buttered 8-inch pan

Cook the dough for 10 minutes

Add flour and milk to the sautéing veggies to form a thick roux

Taste for seasoning while you preheat the oven

Scoop the cool sauce into based and cover with a lattice design

Brush with eggs and cook in the oven until golden brown

Remove when cool and serve

3. Jurassic Park Spicy Goat Soup

"Where is the goat?" She asked. They heard tremors around, and the goat was missing too. Who did it?

Serve 5

Cooking time 90 minutes

Ingredients

- 2 kilograms freshly cut goat meat with skin on
- 2 tbsp tomato paste
- 1 tbsp chili flakes
- ½ tbsp mixed African pepper soup spice
- 2 liters of water
- Salt and beef cube to taste
- 1 tbsp clove basil leaves, chopped

Method

Place cooked goat pieces in a pot

Add the remaining ingredients and allow it to cook until soft

Add the clove basil leaves and serve

4. T-Rex BBQ Steak

A big, ferocious animal with a large appetite for meat, we know this portion will do some justice at dinner.

Serve 2

Cook Time 30 minutes

Ingredients

- 2 large steaks
- 1 dollop of butter
- 1 tbsp crushed garlic
- Fresh thyme sprigs
- ½ freshly squeezed lemon juice
- ¼ cup white sugar
- 1/8 cup tobacco sauce
- Salt and pepper to taste

Methods

Mix the entire ingredient until well incorporated

Soak the steak in for 2 hours or more

Heat up the grill, set steak on the grill until cooked as you like it about 20 minutes or more for well done

Serve with fries or cooked veggies

5. Brachiosaurus Broccoli and cauliflower Salad

The Brachiosaurus is a funny looking dinosaur with long front legs than the hind leg. These herbivores were tall, large, and fed on coniferous trees and shrubs. This salad should be right up to its ally.

Serves 6

Cook Time 25 minutes

Ingredients

- 1 large head of cauliflower, broken up
- 3 cups of broccoli
- 2 cups chopped sweet apples
- ½ cup mayonnaise
- 1 tbsp honey
- ½ tbsp lemon juice
- Freshly ground black pepper
- ½ cup toasted pecans, walnuts, and dried cranberries

Method

Mix the mayo, honey, lemon, black pepper in a large bowl

Add the broccoli, apples, and cauliflower florets

Toss to mix

Add the toasted nuts and cranberries

Chill until ready to serve

6. Jurassic Park Beef Jerky

He ran into the toilet, leaving the kids, but the dinosaur found him. This beef jerky takes inspiration from the coarse skin texture of the T-Rex.

Serve 6

Cook Time 8 hours

Ingredients

- 1 kilogram thinly sliced beef
- 1 tbsp chili flakes
- Salt
- 1 tsp garlic and ginger

Methods

Season the beef properly, and place in the refrigerator to marinate for 2 hours

Arrange them over the dehydrator and allow it to dry over a 110 degree Fahrenheit

Store, and snack on lazy days

7. Stegosaurus Ox Tail Stew

These dinosaurs had a row of bony armored plates running down their spine, and this simple recipe will serve them well.

Serves 6

Cook Time 90 minutes

Ingredients

- 2 kilogram chopped oxtail
- 1 cup chopped onions, carrot, and celery
- 3 cup large diced potato chunks
- 1 can of tomato sauce
- ¼ cup chopped scotch pepper
- ½ tbsp crushed garlic
- Fresh thyme and oregano chopped
- 1 pack beef stock
- Seasoning of choice
- Salt and pepper

Method

Into a crockpot, add a little oil and brown the seasoned oxtail

Remove and cook the onion, chopped pepper, celery, carrots to bring out their flavor

Add the oxtail, tomato sauce, herbs, potatoes, and stock

Season well and leave to slowly cook for 70 minutes

Serve with a sprinkle of parsley

8. Carnotaurus Meat Loaf

The Carnotaurus or horned dinosaur is another carnivore in the family but smaller in size with even shorter front limbs. It is a powerful creature that uses its tail for stability.

Serves 4

Cook Time 50 minutes

Ingredients

- 750 grams ground lean beef
- ½ cup chopped onions
- 1 cup panko breadcrumbs
- 1 tsp Italian seasoning
- 1 egg, beaten
- A dash of vegetable oil
- 1 tsp soy sauce
- 4 tbsp ketchup
- Salt and pepper

Method

Mix everything together except the ketchup

Portion into two small bread pans and rub the top with ketchup to prevent it from drying out

Bake in the oven until done

Allow to rest and slice

9. Compsongnathus German Bratkartoffeln-Pan-fried Potato

These dinosaurs were discovered in Germany and France in the 18th century. We figured if they came to visit, a taste of home should tickle their memory of the good old day.

Serves 6

Cook Time 40 minutes

Ingredients

- 1-ton potatoes, peeled and chopped
- 2 medium-sized onions, chopped
- 9 strips of bacon
- 2 tbsp vegetable oil
- Salt and pepper to taste

Methods

In a large pan, fry the bacon until all the fat is fried off

Remove and crumble and set aside

Add the oil, onions, and seasoning until it is caramelized

Add the potatoes and stir until it is slight brown

Add the bacon crumbs, a dash of paprika, chopped parsley

serve

10. Roasted summer Vegetables Soup

Daniel is trying to climb down a hill but has a little dino buddy looking to play. It is pouring, they are both cold, and we think this colorful soup will keep them warm.

Serves 2

Cook Time 30 minutes

Ingredients

- 4 slices Bacon
- 1 small onion diced
- 1 cup chopped celery
- 1 cup carrot diced
- 2 cups squash diced
- Full cream as desire
- Salt and pepper to taste

Method

Render the fat from the bacon until it is crisp and brown

Set aside, use the oil to coat the veggies and roast in the oven until soft

Pour all the veggies in a blender and puree

Pour the puree in a pot and bring to a simmer

Scoop a spoonful into a bowl, add cream and sprinkle with crushed bacon

serve

11. Baryonyx Tempura Battered Fried Fish

The Baryonyx is a long tail lizard that walks on two legs and loves fishing. This dinosaur loves to fish, and we have one simple, delicious recipe that it will love.

Serves 4

Cook Time 40 minutes

Ingredients

- 8 fillets of white firm fish –cod preferably
- 2 sachet tempura batter mix
- 1 tsp garlic powder
- ½ cup of carbonated drink
- Salt and pepper
- Oil for frying

Method

Heat the oil up

Season the fish with salt and pepper

Pour the tempura batter into a bowl and mix with the carbonated drink

Add the fish one at a time and into the fryer

Fry until brown and serve with some fries

12. Hadrosaurids pan and oven roasted crunchy Skin Duck Breast

These duck-billed dinosaurs are so-called because of the shape of their mouth; the unique feature was their ability to walk on their two hind legs or on all four.

Serve 6

Cook Time 25 minutes

Ingredients

- 2 pounds duck breasts
- 1 tbsp butter unsalted
- Salt and pepper

Method

Preheat oven

Pat the duck breast dry and score the skin but don't cut the flesh

Season generously with salt and pepper

In a pan, add the butter and place the duck skin side down to render the fat until the skin is crunchy about 10 minutes

Flip to the fleshy side and cook in the oven for another 10 minutes

Allow the duck to rest before slicing, serve with sweet cherry sauce

13. Abelisaurus Chicken Kebab

These dinosaurs have the same character as the T-Rex but smaller, and it loves meat too. This spicy and sweet chicken kebab will serve it well.

Serve 4

Cook Time 25 minutes

Ingredients

- 500 grams chicken breast cut into bite-size cubes
- 1 tbsp honey
- 1 tbsp soy sauce
- 1 tbsp hot pepper sauce
- 1 tbsp oil
- 1 tsp crushed garlic and ginger
- 8 metal skewers

Methods

Mix the chicken bits with all the ingredients and allow it to seat for 30 to 60 minutes

Skewer the pieces on and grill until cooked about 6 to 8 minutes

Drizzle a mix of honey, soy sauce, and pepper sauce over it and enjoy

14. Albertosaurus Meat and Veggies Sauce

These meat-eating monsters also had a gentle side to them, and they loved plants too. Guess they needed to be healthy to do all the running to capture their prey.

Serve 4

Cook Time 40 minutes

Ingredients

- 2-pound beef chunks
- 1 tbsp olive oil
- 1 cup onions, celery, and carrot chunks
- 1 can of cannellini beans and sweet corn
- 1 tsp oregano, Italian seasoning, salt, and black pepper
- 1-liter beef or veggie stock

Method

Toss all the veggies with oil and seasoning

Stir fry until partially charred

Remove and sauté the beef chucks

Add the veggies back and add the stock

Add the herb and taste to balance the seasoning

Cook until meat is soft; add the beans and corn for 5 minutes

Serve with mashed potatoes, rice or alone

15. Coelophysis Mini Cookie Nibbles

This dinosaur is among the earliest discovered in the family. It is small, swift, and dashes around easily due to its petite size. Since it won't be staying that long for a visit, this cookie bits should serve it well.

Serves a lot

Cook Time 20 minutes

Ingredients

- 1 pound shortbread cookie dough store-bought
- ½ cup of chocolate chips
- Different shapes small cookie cutter
- 2 tbsp flour

Method

Sprinkle flour on a dry, clean surface

Roll out the dough until it's a ¼ inch thick

Use the cookie cutter to cut out different shapes

Arrange on a lined baking tray and add a chocolate chip to each one

Bake until the edges start to brown or the cookies are brown

Allow to cook and set aside

16. Jurassic Park Spicy Chicken Wings

Only Mr. Arnold's arm survived, but these chicken wings are to die for. They are sweet, sour, and spicy for your taste buds and the dinosaurs too.

Serves 4

Cook Time 50 minutes

Ingredients

- 2 pounds chicken wings – wings and drumettes
- 1 tsp garlic, ginger, and onion powder
- 2 tsp oil
- 1 tbsp honey
- 1 tbsp soy sauce
- 1 tsp chili flakes
- 1 cup flour seasoned with salt and pepper
- Oil to fry

Method

marinate chicken with the ingredients except for the flour and oil

Allow it to marinate for 30 minutes to overnight

Coat on flour and fry until crisp and done

Serve with honey mustard sauce

17. Allosaurus Squid and spaghetti recipe

Another meat-eating dinosaur with an eye in the Barosaurus – a long neck vegetarian dinosaur, this lizard although small, had eyes for big, long things.

Serves 4

Cook Time 40 minutes

Ingredients

- 1-500 grams spaghetti pack
- 2 pounds squid tentacles, cut in 1-inch rounds and cleaned
- 500ml semi-crushed tomatoes
- 1 tbsp fresh chopped pepper
- ½ tsp grated garlic
- 2 tbsp olive oil
- Oregano and parsley as desired
- Salt and pepper

Method

Boil the spaghetti as directed on the pack

While it is cooking, sauté garlic and pepper with oregano until fragrant

Add the tomatoes to cook for 5 minutes then add the squid rounds until it turns opaque about 4 minutes

Taste for seasoning, toss the drained pasta into the sauce, add a little pasta liquid

Sprinkle some parsley and serve

18. Dinosaurs Eggs Caramel Marshmallow Coated Rice Crisp

Dinosaurs laid eggs, large eggs with soft squiggle baby dinosaur that turn out to be fierce as they grew up. This is something kids will love.

Serve 4

Prep Time 30 minutes

Ingredients

- 1 pack of marshmallow
- 1 cup of colored sprinkles
- 1 can of caramel sauce
- 4 cups rice Krispies

Method

Arrange 12 marshmallow balls on a lined tray

Pour over the caramel sauce to coat the marshmallows

Mix rice Krispies and sprinkler in a bowl

Stick a colorful straw into the marshmallow and roll it in the rice Krispies mix

Place into the freezer until firm

Serve it

19. Apatosaurus Berries and Yogurt delight with crunchy nut toppings

This dinosaur is herbivores and loves plants, but it also eats stones to aid digestion. So, this fruit and yogurt delight should clean its insides before the next meals.

Serves 4

Cook Time 30 minutes

Ingredients

- 1 cup mix nuts – anyone you like
- Fruit pack – strawberry, blueberries, and blackberries
- ¼ cup of sugar
- 1 tbsp lemon juice
- 1 can of unsweetened yogurt

Methods

Take four glasses and scoop some yogurt until ¾ cup full

In a pan, cook the berries with a little sugar and lemon until partially melted and cooled

Scoop a spoonful over the chilled yogurt

Add the nuts, a spoon and serve

20. Archaeopteryx Oven Roasted Chicken

The Archaeopteryx is a bird-like dinosaur probably because it can fly and glide too. May not be the great looking among the creatures, but a good roast should brighten it up.

Serves 8

Cook Time 45 minutes

Ingredients

- 2 pounds whole chicken, cleaned and dried
- 1 tbsp grated ginger
- 1 tbsp grated garlic
- 2 tbsp unsalted butter
- Salt and black pepper

Method

Preheat the oven

Pat the bird dry and place on an oven tray

Mix the remaining ingredient

Generously rub in-between the skin and all bird

Cook in the oven until skin is crispy and the water runs clear

21. Deinonychus chicken feet snack

The Deinonychus was a small, speedy dinosaur with funny-looking feet, hence the inspiration. It had feathers around front limbs, which could be why they moved so fast.

Serves 4

Cooking time 40 minutes

Ingredients

- 1 kg chicken feet, cleaned
- ½ cup chopped white onion
- 1 tsp garlic
- 1 tsp ginger
- 1 tsp finely chopped fresh pepper
- ¼ cup of soy sauce
- 2 tbsp honey
- Salt and pepper

Method

Place chicken feet in a pot; add all the ingredients except for the soy sauce and honey

Let it cook until soft, fluffy, and the stock is almost dried

Add the soy and honey, and reduce to a simmer

Let it form a sticky coating, pour in a bowl

serve

22. Diplodocus Hummus Dipping Sauce

What better sauce for a dinosaur that replaced its teeth every 32 days despite its diet of plants. So, we are sure it will love this dipping sauce with some veggies to go too.

Serves 4

Cook Time 20 minutes

Ingredients

- 50 grams cooked garbanzo beans
- 120 grams Tahini
- 25 grams ground white sesame seeds
- ½ tbsp garlic
- ½ tsp paprika
- ½ tsp crushed chill
- ½ tbsp cumin
- Salt to taste
- 1 tbsp olive oil

Method

Blend all the ingredients until soft and creamy in a mixer

Scoop into a bowl

Sprinkle some crushed chili over

Drizzle some oil to prevent it from drying

Serve with veggies – carrot, celery, taco chips

23. Dinosaur Braised beef shanks

We are also wondered at the bull on a sling been served to the T-Rex in the cage, and dinner could not be better than braised shanks.

Serves 6

Cook Time 75 minutes

Ingredients

- 2 kilogram beef on the bone
- 2 cups chopped onions
- 1 cup chopped celery
- ¼ cup of grated garlic
- 1000ml beef broth
- 3 cups of your favorite red wine
- 3 bay leaves
- Salt and pepper
- 1 cup apple cider vinegar
- 2 cups carrots

Method

In a slow cooker, braised seasoned beef shanks in 2 tsp of oil

Remove and cook all the vegetables

Add the shanks back, add the wine, bay leaves, cider, broths, taste for seasoning and allow to cook

Beef should be tender and falling of the bone when done

serve

24. Giganotosaurus Banoffee Pie

Did you know that the Giganotosaurus, despite its size, has a very small brain? But it was a very smart hunter with itineraries to match the T-Rex.

Serves 4

Cook Time 30 minutes

Ingredient

- 2 tbsp melted salted butter
- 1 small can dulce de leche
- 3 medium-size banana, peeled and cut in circles
- 2 cups crushed digestive biscuits
- 300 grams unsweetened whipped cream
- Toasted nuts for extra crunch

Method

Mix the biscuit crumbs, and butter to form the base of the pie pressing with your fingers to form a firm bottom

Bake in an oven until it is brown and cook to give it the crunchy base

Allow to cool completely, add the dulce de leche to cover the base, be generous

Arrange the banana slices all over the caramel

Place in a refrigerator

Whipped the cream until stiff peaks are formed

Scoop into a piping bag and make a beautiful circular pattern

Sprinkle the nuts, chill, and serve or blowtorch to add color

25. Minmi White Chocolate chips Cupcake

This is another member of the heavily plated spiky dinosaurs but faster than others in the family. This recipe is a replica of how it looks on the outside, and we know it will love it.

Serves 6

Cook Time 30 minutes

Ingredients

- 250-gram butter
- 200 grams of sugar
- 200 grams self-rising flour
- 2 large eggs
- ¼ cup evaporated milk
- ½ cup white chocolate chips

Method

Cream butter with sugar until creamy and fluffy

Add the milk and eggs one at a time, beating in low

Add the flour using the folding technique

Add the chocolate chips and scoop into cupcake lined pan

Bake for 15 minutes or until a skewer comes out clean

Add icing if you like or enjoy with a cool glass of juice.

26. Spinosaurus BBQ Baby Back Pork Ribs

This meat-eating dinosaur is larger than the T-Rex. It had a sail-like feature across its back covered in spines hence the names.

Serves 5

Cook Time 90 minutes

Ingredients

- 2 baby back pork ribs about 6 pounds
- 1 cup BBQ sauce
- 1 tbsp onion powder, garlic powder
- 2 tbsp sugar
- ½ cup apple paste
- Juice of a lemon
- ¼ tsp tobacco sauce or more if you like spice
- 1 tsp paprika
- Fresh thyme sprigs
- Salt and freshly crushed black pepper

Method

Pat the ribs dry

Massage all the ingredients on the ribs both sides

Allow it to sit for 30 minutes

On a smoker, grilled ribs until soft, tender, and just about falling apart

Keep rubbing the mix as it is cooking

Remove from the grill, chop into section and enjoy

27. T-Rex Stir-fry Shrimps

Perhaps it's the most popular dinosaurs and a meat lover, but these shrimps are big on flavors and one that will entice the senses.

Serves 4

Cook Time 25 minutes

Ingredient

- 1 pound giant shrimps, peeled, deveined with tail on
- ¼ cup finely chopped onions
- 1 tsp fresh garlic
- ½ tsp grated ginger
- 1 tbsp lemon juice
- 1 tbsp sweet orange juice
- 1 tbsp olive oil
- Fresh chives

Method

In a pan, sauté the onions add the shrimp and all the ingredients except the chives

Allow it to cook for 4 minutes until pink

Add the chives for a minute

serve

28. Troodon Baked Nut Crusted Salmon

Troodon was a dinosaur family with long claws, speed, and a predator in its own class and regarded as omnivores. They were avid hunters who ate fruits, soft plants, and seeds.

Serves 4

Cooked Time 25 minutes

Ingredients

- 4 salmon steaks
- ½ cup chopped fresh seedless dates
- ½ cup of crushed cashew nuts
- ½ cup of plain breadcrumbs
- 1 tsp oregano, thyme, and basil
- 1 tbsp grainy mustard
- Salt and pepper

Method

Season salmon with salt and pepper

Butter generously with mustard

Mix remaining ingredients and layer on one side of the salmon

Bake in a preheated oven for 10 -15 minutes

Serves with veggies and a slice of lemon

29. Dinosaur shaped cookies

The kids had fun running around exploring the different dinosaurs in Jurassic Park, and they deserve a treat, would you say? These are the best too.

Makes a lot

Cook Time 40 minutes

Ingredients

- 2 cups flour, double sifted
- 1 large egg
- 2 tbsp butter
- 1 cup of sugar
- 2 tbsp brown sugar
- ½ tsp baking powder
- 1 tsp vanilla extract
- 12o ml milk

Method

Add all the ingredients in a bowl and form dough

Flatten the dough with a roller

Use dino shape cutters to cut the shapes

Align on a baking tray, bake until edges are brown

Remove to cool, store, and enjoy

30. Jurassic Park Adult Cocktail

After all the running and adventure, a good drink will calm the nerve and relax you for the premiere of the movie?

Serve 2

Prep Time 10 minutes

Ingredients

- 1 cup of coconut water
- ¼ cup vodka
- 2 cups freshly made lemonade
- 1 cup punch
- Cherrie and olive on a stick
- Ice cubes

Method

Add the ingredient in a large shaker and mix well

Pour into a glass with an ice cube and serve

For the kids, omit the vodka.

Conclusion

What an adventure? We learned about different dinosaurs, tried out new delicious recipes that the whole family can enjoy, and still got time to watch the movie. If you haven't watched the movie, please do. If you have watched the adventure, then enjoy cooking these dinosaur meals with your kids while educating them about a piece of our history that is extinct.

About the Author

Susan Gray is a restaurateur and writer born in Maui, Hawaii, and spent the first 18 years of her life there. Her first step in cooking was influenced by her mother who managed a catering company and involved her in lots of her cooking. That experience was the eye-opener for her.

When she left home for college, she worked briefly in the kitchen of a restaurant close to her college, where she was studying to have a degree in nutrition and dietetics at The Steinhardt School of Culture, Education, and Human Development. Her experiences at the restaurant, coupled with her degree laid the map before her.

She stayed in New York after her degree, where she met her husband. Together, they started their restaurant business, and it hit the roof. Susan, however, felt that there was more to do. She figured that she could help people discover and unlock the many tastes and experiences associated with cooking. She decided to write as much as she can to help people get the best out of their diet through food.

She has since been writing and publishing categories of recipes in a host of online and offline publications. And she is having absolute fun doing so.

Author's Afterthoughts

In the beginning, I wasn't quite sure if I should take the plunge and write this book. But I thought that there might be people out there who are looking for this sort of thing, and I would be failing them if I don't get down and get this thing out. See? You, my dear reader, made me do this. That's how much power you have.

I'm excited and humbled that you went for this book out of all the options available. It's nothing short of gratifying.

I would like to hear back from you. What do you think about this book? Please leave your comments as a review on Amazon. It would mean a whole lot to me.

Thank you for being so awesome.

Susan Gray

Made in the USA
Middletown, DE
14 November 2020